GAPS DIET

MEGA BUNDLE – 4 Manuscripts in 1 – 160+ GAPS - friendly recipes including breakfast, side dishes, and desserts for a delicious and tasty diet

TABLE OF CONTENTS

Committee of Publishers and Associations.

Introduction

GAPS recipes for personal enjoyment but also for family enjoyment. You will love them for sure for how easy it is to prepare them.

ROAST RECIPES

ROASTED SQUASH

Serves: **3-4**

Prep Time: **10** Minutes

Cook Time: **20** Minutes

Total Time: **30** Minutes

INGREDIENTS

- 2 delicata squashes
- 2 tablespoons olive oil
- 1 tsp curry powder
- 1 tsp salt

DIRECTIONS

1. Preheat the oven to 400 F
2. Cut everything in half lengthwise
3. Toss everything with olive oil and place onto a prepared baking sheet
4. Roast for 18-20 minutes at 400 F or until golden brown
5. When ready remove from the oven and serve

ROASTED CUCUMBER

Serves: **3-4**

Prep Time: **10**   Minutes

Cook Time: **20**   Minutes

Total Time: **30**   Minutes

INGREDIENTS

- 2 lb. cucumber
- 2 tablespoons olive oil
- 1 tsp curry powder
- 1 tsp salt

DIRECTIONS

1. Preheat the oven to 400 F
2. Cut everything in half lengthwise
3. Toss everything with olive oil and place onto a prepared baking sheet
4. Roast for 18-20 minutes at 400 F or until golden brown
5. When ready remove from the oven and serve

ZUCCHINI SOUP

Serves: **4**

Prep Time: **10**   Minutes

Cook Time: **20**   Minutes

Total Time: **30**   Minutes

INGREDIENTS

- 1 tablespoon olive oil
- 1 lb. zucchini
- ¼ red onion
- ½ cup all-purpose flour
- ¼ tsp salt
- ¼ tsp pepper
- 1 can vegetable broth
- 1 cup heavy cream

DIRECTIONS

1. In a saucepan heat olive oil and sauté zucchini until tender
2. Add remaining ingredients to the saucepan and bring to a boil
3. When all the vegetables are tender transfer to a blender and blend until smooth
4. Pour soup into bowls, garnish with parsley and serve

BEAN SOUP

Serves: **4**

Prep Time: **10**   Minutes

Cook Time: **230**   Minutes

Total Time: **240**   Minutes

INGREDIENTS

- 2 cups beans
- 1/2 tsp salt
- 2 cups chicken broth
- 7 cups water
- 2 tsp sauce
- ½ 10-ounce package onions
- 2 clove garlic
- 3 bay leaves
- ½ tsp dried rosemary
- 1 tsp dried sage
- 2 tsp dried thyme

DIRECTIONS

1. Place the bean mixture in a pot with the rest of ingredients
2. Cook over medium heat until the soup boils
3. Reduce the heat and simmer for 3-4 hours

4. When ready remove from heat and serve

SIDE DISHES

RICE PAPER ROLLS

Serves: **4**

Prep Time: **10**   Minutes

Cook Time: **15**   Minutes

Total Time: **25**   Minutes

INGREDIENTS

- 1 cucumber
- 1 red capsicum
- 1 carrot
- 1 avocado
- 2 oz. pea sprouts
- ¾ coriander
- ¾ cup mint
- 2 oz. peanuts
- 2 tablespoons chili sauce
- 1 tablespoon soy sauce
- 2 tablespoons lime juice

DIRECTIONS

1. Place all the vegetables on a plate
2. In a bowl mix chili sauce, lime juice and soy sauce

3. Some one rice paper roll in a bowl of water and then place vegetables on the wrapper

4. Fold up the bottom of the wrapped, and roll u to enclose filling

5. Place on a tray, serve with dipping sauce

Serves: *4*

Prep Time: *10*   Minutes

Cook Time: *30*   Minutes

Total Time: *40*   Minutes

INGREDIENTS

- 1 lb. tenderloins
- 2 oz. rice noodle
- 1 carrot
- 1 celery stalk
- 1 cucumber
- ¼ capsicum
- 1 tablespoon peanuts

DRESSING

- 1 onion
- 1 garlic clove
- ½ cup soy sauce
- ½ cup rice vinegar
- 1 tsp sugar
- 1 tsp sesame oil

DIRECTIONS

1. Place all dressing ingredients in a jar and mix well
2. In a bowl place all salad ingredients and mix well
3. Pour dressing over salad and serve

SHREDDED SWEET POTATO HASH BROWNS

Serves: **2**
Prep Time: **10**   minutes
Cook Time: **30**   minutes
Total Time: **40**   minutes

INGREDIENTS

- 7 oz. sweet potatoes
- 3 tablespoons butter
- 1 tablespoon dried sage
- 1/8 tablespoon black pepper
- 1/8 tablespoon salt

DIRECTIONS

1. Shred the potatoes and place them in a strainer.
2. Use a rubber spatula and press the excess water.
3. Place the potatoes on a paper towel and pat as dry as possible.
4. Put the potatoes in a bowl and add sage, salt and pepper.
5. Place the butter in a skillet over high heat.
6. When the butter is melted add the potatoes.
7. Toss well for 5 minutes and gather them together into two piles.
8. Cook the potatoes slowly.
9. Cook on each side for 3 minutes.

Serves: **2**

Prep Time: **10** minutes

Cook Time: **35** minutes

Total Time: **45** minutes

INGREDIENTS

- 4 quarts' water
- 5 meatballs
- ½ tomato sauce
- ½ ounces Parmigiano-Reggiano
- 2 ounces' spaghetti noodles

DIRECTIONS

1. In a large pot add water to high heat
2. Add spaghetti noodles
3. Add the meatballs and tomato sauce in a medium sauce pan while the pasta is cooking
4. Remove the noodles and allow them to drain
5. Place the noodles in the sauce with the meatballs

HOMEMADE CHICKEN NUGGETS

Serves: **4**

Prep Time: **10** Minutes

Cook Time: **30** Minutes

Total Time: **40** Minutes

INGREDIENTS

- 1 lbs. chicken breast
- 2 small eggs
- ¼ tsp garlic powder
- ¼ tsp salt
- ¼ cup breadcrumbs
- 1 ½ cups cauliflower

DIRECTIONS

1. Preheat oven to 325 F and place a baking tray in
2. In a bowl mix garlic powder, salt and egg and whisk together
3. In another bowl mix cauliflower and breadcrumbs, dip the chicken into the mixture
4. Bake for 20-25 minutes on each side

GRILLED VEGETABLES

Serves: **4**

Prep Time: **10**   Minutes

Cook Time: **10**   Minutes

Total Time: **20**   Minutes

INGREDIENTS

- 1 tablespoon olive oil
- ¼ tsp salt
- 2 bell peppers
- 1 bunch asparagus
- 2 small zucchinis
- 1 tablespoon rice vinegar
- 1 tablespoon oregano
- 1 eggplant

DIRECTIONS

1. In a bowl whisk salt, oregano, vinegar and olive oil
2. Place the vegetables into a bowl
3. Place vegetables on a grill
4. Cook eggplant and zucchini pieces for 5-6 minutes per side
5. Toss asparagus and cool for 4-5 minutes
6. Transfer to a plate and serve when ready

PORK KEBABS

Serves: *8*

Prep Time: *10*   Minutes

Cook Time: *15*   Minutes

Total Time: *25*   Minutes

INGREDIENTS

- ½ cup fresh basil
- 22 red globe grapes
- ¼ Tsp allspice
- 1 lb. pork loin chop
- 1 tsp cumin
- ¼ tsp cardamom
- ¼ tsp salt
- 2 tsp fenugreek seeds
- ¼ black pepper

DIRECTIONS

1. In a bowl mix cumin, cardamom, salt, pepper, fenugreek and set aside
2. Cut the pork and sprinkle the mixture onto the pork cubes and stir until well coated
3. For each kebab slide a cube of pork into the skewer and alternate with basil wrapped grapes

4. Preheat the grill and cook for 10-15 minutes

TUNA PASTA SALAD

Serves: **4**

Prep Time: **10**   Minutes

Cook Time: **30**   Minutes

Total Time: **40**   Minutes

INGREDIENTS

- 3 cups bow tie pasta
- 1 cup cherry tomatoes
- 1 tablespoon olive oil
- 2 tablespoons wine vinegar
- 1 tsp mustard
- ¼ cup parsley
- 1 tin tuna

DIRECTIONS

1. Combine all ingredients together and mix well
2. Serve when ready

ROASTED CHICKPEAS

Serves: **4**

Prep Time: **10** Minutes

Cook Time: **30** Minutes

Total Time: **40** Minutes

INGREDIENTS

- 2 cans chickpeas
- 1 tsp olive oil
- 1 tsp salt
- 1 tsp pepper
- 1 tsp thyme
- 1 tsp rosemary

DIRECTIONS

1. Preheat oven to 350 F
2. Line an oven tray with baking paper, toss chickpeas in salt, pepper and oil
3. Pour mixture over baking paper and roast for 20-25 minutes
4. Remove and serve

Serves: **3**

Prep Time: **10** Minutes

Cook Time: **10** Minutes

Total Time: **20** Minutes

INGREDIENTS

- 1 tablespoon avocado oil
- 3 carrots
- 3 large nori sheets
- 1 tomato
- 1 tablespoon fresh cilantro
- 1 red pepper
- 1 green bell pepper
- 1 while onion
- 1 jalapeno

DIRECTIONS

1. In a skillet sauce avocado oil, onion, jalapeno, white onion, salt and pepper for 6-7 minutes
2. Remove from heat and place mixture in a bowl
3. Sauté carrots with pepper and salt for 5-6 minutes
4. Combine coconut milk with curry powder and combine with red onion, sea s alt and pepper

5. Lay the nori sheets and top with pepper mixture and carrots and drizzle with coconut milk

FISH TACOS

Serves: **4**

Prep Time: **10** Minutes

Cook Time: **30** Minutes

Total Time: **40** Minutes

INGREDIENTS

- 8 fish fingers
- ¼ cabbage
- tacos
- guacamole
- 2 avocados
- salt
- coriander
- juice of 1 lime

Salsa

- 2 cherry tomatoes
- ½ onion
- 1 tablespoon vinegar
- 8 jalapeno slices
- juice 1 lime
- salt

Spicy mayo

- ½ cup mayo

- 1 tablespoon paprika
- ½ cup ketchup
- juice 1 lime

DIRECTIONS

1. For salsa add all the ingredients into a blender and blend until smooth, place into a bowl and set aside
2. Mash avocado with salt, lime juice and mix with coriander
3. Mix your spicy mayo in a bowl, heat your tacos and pour the mixture on the tacos
4. Serve when ready

AVOCADO SANDWICH

Serves: **1**

Prep Time: **10** Minutes

Cook Time: **10** Minutes

Total Time: **20** Minutes

INGREDIENTS

- 1 avocado
- juice of 1 lemon pinch of salt
- coriander
- 6 rashers of bacon
- 4 slices bread
- 2 eggs
- ¼ tablespoon hot sauce

DIRECTIONS

1. In a pan add bacon and cook over medium heat
2. In a bowl mix lemon juice, salt, avocado and coriander
3. Toss your bread in the pan and crack an egg into the bread (make a hole before)
4. Add the avocado mixture over the bread and top with bacon

GREEN PESTO PASTA

Serves: 2
Prep Time: 5   Minutes
Cook Time: 15   Minutes
Total Time: 20   Minutes

INGREDIENTS

- 4 oz. spaghetti
- 2 cups basil leaves
- 2 garlic cloves
- ¼ cup olive oil
- 2 tablespoons parmesan cheese
- ½ tsp black pepper

DIRECTIONS

1. Bring water to a boil and add pasta
2. In a blend add parmesan cheese, basil leaves, garlic and blend
3. Add olive oil, pepper and blend again
4. Pour pesto onto pasta and serve when ready

CAULIFLOWER STEAKS WITH LEMON SAUCE

Serves: **4**

Prep Time: **10**   Minutes

Cook Time: **10**   Minutes

Total Time: **20**   Minutes

INGREDIENTS

- 1 head cauliflower
- 2 tablespoons olive oil
- 2 tsp paprika

LEMON SAUCE

- 1 cup parsley leaves
- ¼ cup mint leaves
- 1 garlic clove
- ¼ cup olive oil
- ¼ cup green onion
- Juice of 1 lemon

DIRECTIONS

1. In a blender add all ingredients for the lemon sauce and blend until smooth
2. For the cauliflower steak, cut cauliflower into thick slices and rub with olive oil

3. Sprinkle with spices and place the cauliflower in a skillet
4. Cook for 4-5 minutes per side
5. When ready remove and serve with lemon sauce

Serves: **4**

Prep Time: **10** Minutes

Cook Time: **30** Minutes

Total Time: **40** Minutes

INGREDIENTS

- 2 tablespoons olive oil
- salt
- 2 scallions
- ¼ cup cilantro
- 1 head cauliflower
- 1 tablespoon sesame seeds

SAUCE

- 1 tablespoon rice wine vinegar
- 1 tablespoon ginger
- 1 tsp olive oil
- 1 tablespoon soy sauce
- 1 tablespoon hoisin sauce

DIRECTIONS

1. In a bowl combine all sauce ingredients together and mix well
2. For the cauliflower heat the olive oil in a skillet and add the cauliflower

3. Add salt, sesame seeds and cook for 4-5 minutes
4. When ready remove from heat, add cilantro and stir to combine
5. Serve with sauce

RICE, KALE AND AVOCADO BOWL

Serves: **2**

Prep Time: **10**   Minutes

Cook Time: **20**   Minutes

Total Time: **30**   Minutes

INGREDIENTS

- 1 cup rice
- 1 garlic clove
- 1 tablespoon rice vinegar
- 2 cups vegetable broth
- pinch of salt
- pinch of pepper
- 2 tablespoons
- 1 bunch kale
- 1 bunch kale
- 1 avocado

DIRECTIONS

1. In a pot stir in broth, rice and garlic
2. Bring to a simmer for and cook until liquid is evaporated
3. When ready toss rice with salt, pepper and vinegar
4. In another books toss kale with olive oil

5. Add kale and avocado slices to the rice

6. Serve when ready

CHICKEN MEATBALLS AND CAULIFLOWER RICE

Serves: *4*

Prep Time: *10*   Minutes

Cook Time: *30*   Minutes

Total Time: *40*   Minutes

INGREDIENTS

- ¼ cup red onion
- 1 lb. ground chicken
- 1 tablespoon mustard
- ¼ tsp black pepper
- 1 tablespoon olive oil
- 1 garlic clove
- ¼ cup parsley
- pinch of salt

SAUCE

- 1 cup parsley
- 1 can coconut milk
- 2 scallions
- zest of 1 lemon
- 1 cup ready-made cauliflower rice

DIRECTIONS

1. In a skillet heat olive oil and sauté onion and garlic for 3-4 minutes
2. Remove sautéed onion and garlic to a bowl
3. Stir in parsley, mustard, chicken, seasoning and mix well
4. Form balls from the mixture and place on a baking sheet
5. Bake at 400 F for 20 minutes
6. When ready remove from the oven and set aside
7. In a blender add all ingredients for the sauce and blend
8. Top the meatballs with sauce and cauliflower rice and serve

PINEAPPLE CHICKEN AND LETTUCE WRAPS

Serves: *2*

Prep Time: *10*   Minutes

Cook Time: *20*   Minutes

Total Time: *30*   Minutes

INGREDIENTS

- 2 cups cooked chicken
- 1 tablespoon olive oil
- ¼ tsp paprika
- 1 tablespoon lime juice
- ¼ tsp garlic powder
- ¼ tsp salt
- 1 cup pineapple cubes
- 8 lettuce wraps

DIRECTIONS

1. In a bowl combine garlic powder, lime juice, paprika, olive oil and lime juice
2. In your lettuce wraps add pineapple cubes, chicken and top with lime mixture
3. Serve when ready

Serves: **4**

Prep Time: **10**   Minutes

Cook Time: **35**   Minutes

Total Time: **45**   Minutes

INGREDIENTS

- 1 lb. potatoes
- 1 tsp lemon juice
- 4 salmon fillets
- ¼ tsp paprika
- 2 tablespoons olive oil

DIRECTIONS

1. Bake the potatoes at 375 F for 20-25 minutes
2. Rub the salmon fillets with paprika and olive oil
3. Bake the fish until golden brown
4. When ready from the oven and serve with baked potatoes and lemon juice

GUT ENERGY BOOSTING BOWL

Serves: *1*

Prep Time: *5*   Minutes

Cook Time: *5*   Minutes

Total Time: *10* Minutes

INGREDIENTS

- 2 cups kale
- 1 tablespoon olive oil
- 1 avocado
- ¼ cup carrot
- ½ cup beans
- ¼ cup cabbage
- 1 cup baked potatoes

DIRECTIONS

1. In a bowl add all ingredients together
2. Drizzle olive oil and salt and mix well
3. Serve when ready

BALED EGGS WITH ZOODLES

Serves: 2

Prep Time: 5   Minutes

Cook Time: 10   Minutes

Total Time: 15   Minutes

INGREDIENTS

- 2 zucchinis
- pinch of salt
- 2 avocados
- 2 tablespoons olive oil
- 2 eggs
- 1 tablespoon olive oil

DIRECTIONS

1. In a bowl toss the zucchini noodles with olive oil
2. Season and transfer to a baking sheet
3. Crack an egg over each portion
4. Bake for 8-10 minutes at 375 F
5. When ready remove from the oven and serve with avocado slices

CHICKEN WITH BAKED VEGGIES

Serves: **4**

Prep Time: **10** Minutes

Cook Time: **30** Minutes

Total Time: **40** Minutes

INGREDIENTS

- 1 tablespoon olive oil
- 1 tablespoon honey
- 2 red bell peppers
- 2 carrots
- ¼ cup parsley
- 1 lb. chicken breast
- 2 onions

DIRECTIONS

1. Place the chicken onto a baking sheet
2. Add the rest of the ingredients to the chicken breast
3. Drizzle olive oil over chicken and veggies
4. Bake at 375 F for 25-30 minutes or until the vegetables are tender
5. When ready remove from the oven and serve

VEGGIE STIR-FRY

Serves: 2

Prep Time: **10**   Minutes

Cook Time: **20**   Minutes

Total Time: **30**   Minutes

INGREDIENTS

- 1 tablespoon cornstarch
- 1 garlic clove
- ¼ cup olive oil
- ¼ head broccoli
- ¼ cup show peas
- ½ cup carrots
- ¼ cup green beans
- 1 tablespoon soy sauce
- ½ cup onion

DIRECTIONS

1. In a bowl combine garlic, olive oil, cornstarch and mix well
2. Add the rest of the ingredients and toss to coat
3. In a skillet cook vegetables mixture until tender
4. When ready transfer to a plate garnish with ginger and serve

WALDORF SALAD

Serves: **2**

Prep Time: **5**   Minutes

Cook Time: **5**   Minutes

Total Time: **10**   Minutes

INGREDIENTS

- 1 tablespoon mayonnaise
- 1 tablespoon lemon juice
- 1 apple
- 1 cup red grapes
- ½ cup cranberries
- ½ cup walnuts
- 12 cup celery
- 6 lettuce leaves

DIRECTIONS

1. Combine all ingredients together and mix well
2. Serve with dressing

CRANBERRY SALAD

Serves: **2**

Prep Time: **5**   Minutes

Cook Time: **5**   Minutes

Total Time: **10**   Minutes

INGREDIENTS

- 1 can unsweetened pineapple
- 1 package cherry gelatin
- 1 tablespoon lemon juice
- ½ cup artificial sweetener
- 1 cup cranberries
- 1 orange
- 1 cup celery
- ½ cup pecans

DIRECTIONS

1. Combine all ingredients together and mix well
2. Serve with dressing

ARUGULA SALAD

Serves: **1**

Prep Time: **5**   Minutes

Cook Time: **5**   Minutes

Total Time: **10** Minutes

INGREDIENTS

- 2 cups arugula leaves
- ¼ cup cranberries
- ¼ cup honey
- ¼ cup pecans
- 1 cup salad dressing

DIRECTIONS

1. Combine all ingredients together and mix well
2. Serve with dressing

MANDARIN SALAD

Serves: *2*

Prep Time: *10*   Minutes

Cook Time: *20*   Minutes

Total Time: *30*   Minutes

INGREDIENTS

- 2 tsp maple syrup
- 3 tbs oil
- 3 mandarins
- 1 avocado
- 150 g walnuts
- 250 g kale
- 150 g spinach
- 1 lemon
- 150 g Brussels sprouts
- ½ red onion

DIRECTIONS

1. Preheat the oven to 400F
2. Dice the sprouts, red onion, kale and avocado
3. Cut the mandarins
4. Pulse the walnuts just a little using a food processor
5. Mix the walnuts with lemon zest
6. Mix together the maple syrup, oil and lemon juice

7. Add the walnuts to the vegetables, pour the dressing over and serve

BEAN FAJITAS

Serves: *2*
Prep Time: *5*   Minutes

Cook Time: *10*   Minutes

Total Time: *15*   Minutes

INGREDIENTS

- 1 kidney beans can
- Tortillas
- 3 tsp cumin
- 2 tsp garlic powder
- 5 mushrooms
- 2 red peppers
- 2 yellow peppers
- 1 onion

DIRECTIONS

1. Cook the peppers and the onion until caramelized
2. Add the mushrooms, garlic powder and cumin
3. Add the kidney beans after a few minutes when the mushrooms turn brown
4. Cook until soft
5. Heat the tortillas
6. Fill them with the vegetable mixture and serve

TOFU SALAD

Serves: **1**

Prep Time: **5**   Minutes

Cook Time: **5**   Minutes

Total Time: **10** Minutes

INGREDIENTS

- 1 pack tofu
- 1 cup chopped vegetables (carrots, cucumber)

DRESSING

- 1 tablespoon sesame oil
- 1 tablespoon mustard
- 1 tablespoon brown rice vinegar
- 1 tablespoon soya sauce

DIRECTIONS

1. Combine all ingredients together and mix well
2. Add salad dressing, toss well and serve

PAD THAI SALAD

Serves: **1**

Prep Time: **5** Minutes

Cook Time: **5** Minutes

Total Time: **10** Minutes

INGREDIENTS

- ¼ lb. rice noodles
- 1 red pepper
- 1 onion
- 4 stalks coriander
- ¼ package silken tofu
- 1 oz. roasted peanuts
- Salad dressing

DIRECTIONS

1. Combine all ingredients together and mix well
2. Add salad dressing, toss well and serve

STEW RECIPES

BEEF STEW

Serves: **4**

Prep Time: **15** Minutes

Cook Time: **45** Minutes

Total Time: **60** Minutes

INGREDIENTS

- 2 lb. beef
- 1 tsp salt
- 4 tablespoons olive oil
- 2 red onions
- 2 cloves garlic
- 1 cup white wine
- 2 cups beef broth
- 1 cup water
- 3-4 bay leaves
- ¼ tsp thyme
- 1 lb. potatoes

DIRECTIONS

1. Chop all ingredients in big chunks
2. In a large pot heat olive oil and add ingredients one by one
3. Cook for 5-6 or until slightly brown
4. Add remaining ingredients and cook until tender, 35-45 minutes
5. Season while stirring on low heat
6. When ready remove from heat and serve

IRISH STEW

Serves: **4**

Prep Time: **15** Minutes

Cook Time: **45** Minutes

Total Time: **60** Minutes

INGREDIENTS

- 4-5 slices bacon
- 2 lb. beef
- ¼ cup flour
- ½ tsp black pepper
- 4 carrots
- ½ cup beef broth

DIRECTIONS

1. Chop all ingredients in big chunks
2. In a large pot heat olive oil and add ingredients one by one
3. Cook for 5-6 or until slightly brown
4. Add remaining ingredients and cook until tender, 35-45 minutes
5. Season while stirring on low heat
6. When ready remove from heat and serve

CHICKEN CASSEROLE

Serves:	**4**
Prep Time:	**10** Minutes
Cook Time:	**15** Minutes
Total Time:	**25** Minutes

INGREDIENTS

- 1 tablespoon olive oil
- 1 lb. chicken breast
- 1 red onion
- 2 cloves garlic
- 1 tsp paprika
- 4 cups cooked rice
- ¼ cup cranberries
- 1 lb. brussels sprouts
- 1 potato

DIRECTIONS

1. Sauté the veggies and set aside
2. Preheat the oven to 425 F
3. Transfer the sautéed veggies to a baking dish, add remaining ingredients to the baking dish

4. Mix well, add seasoning and place the dish in the oven
5. Bake for 12-15 minutes or until slightly brown
6. When ready remove from the oven and serve

RICE CASSEROLE

Serves: **4**
Prep Time: **10**   Minutes

Cook Time: **15**   Minutes

Total Time: **25**   Minutes

INGREDIENTS

- 2 cups cooked rice
- 1 red onion
- ¼ cup olive oil
- 1 can mushroom soup
- 2 lb. chicken thighs
- 2 tablespoons butter
- 1 clove garlic
- 1 tablespoon parsley

DIRECTIONS

1. Sauté the veggies and set aside
2. Preheat the oven to 425 F
3. Transfer the sautéed veggies to a baking dish, add remaining ingredients to the baking dish
4. Mix well, add seasoning and place the dish in the oven
5. Bake for 12-15 minutes or until slightly brown
6. When ready remove from the oven and serve

MUSHROOM PIZZA

Serves: **2**

Prep Time: **10**   Minutes

Cook Time: **30**   Minutes

Total Time: **40**   Minutes

INGREDIENTS

- 2 button mushrooms
- ½ red onion
- 1 lemon juiced
- 1 tablespoon parsley
- ½ cup ground flax seeds
- 2 tablespoons olive oil
- 1 cup almonds whole
- 1 cup cashews whole
- 1 carrot

DIRECTIONS

1. Preheat oven to 375 F and place a baking sheet
2. In food processor place all the ingredients and blend for 8-10 minutes

3. Pour the mixture on the baking sheet and bake for 15-20 minutes until golden

4. Remove from the oven and serve

CASSEROLE PIZZA

Serves: **6-8**
Prep Time: **10**   Minutes

Cook Time: **15**   Minutes

Total Time: **25**   Minutes

INGREDIENTS

- 1 pizza crust
- ½ cup tomato sauce
- ¼ black pepper
- 1 cup zucchini slices
- 1 cup mozzarella cheese
- 1 cup olives

DIRECTIONS

1. Spread tomato sauce on the pizza crust
2. Place all the toppings on the pizza crust
3. Bake the pizza at 425 F for 12-15 minutes
4. When ready remove pizza from the oven and serve

SECOND COOKBOOK

CAULIFLOWER SOUP

Serves: **4**

Prep Time: **10** Minutes

Cook Time: **20** Minutes

Total Time: **30** Minutes

INGREDIENTS

- 1 tablespoon olive oil
- 1 lb. cauliflower
- ¼ red onion
- ½ cup all-purpose flour
- ¼ tsp salt
- ¼ tsp pepper
- 1 can vegetable broth
- 1 cup heavy cream

DIRECTIONS

1. In a saucepan heat olive oil and sauté cauliflower until tender
2. Add remaining ingredients to the saucepan and bring to a boil
3. When all the vegetables are tender transfer to a blender and blend until smooth
4. Pour soup into bowls, garnish with parsley and serve

Serves: **4**

Prep Time: **10** Minutes

Cook Time: **20** Minutes

Total Time: **30** Minutes

INGREDIENTS

- 1 tablespoon olive oil
- 1 lb. zucchini
- 2 tablespoons garlic
- ¼ red onion
- ½ cup all-purpose flour
- ¼ tsp salt
- ¼ tsp pepper
- 1 can vegetable broth
- 1 cup heavy cream

DIRECTIONS

1. In a saucepan heat olive oil and sauté garlic until tender
2. Add remaining ingredients to the saucepan and bring to a boil
3. When all the vegetables are tender transfer to a blender and blend until smooth
4. Pour soup into bowls, garnish with parsley and serve

LEEK SOUP

Serves: **4**

Prep Time: **10**   Minutes

Cook Time: **20**   Minutes

Total Time: **30**   Minutes

INGREDIENTS

- 1 tablespoon olive oil
- 1 lb. spinach
- ¼ red onion
- ½ cup all-purpose flour
- ¼ tsp salt
- ¼ tsp pepper
- 1 can vegetable broth
- 1 cup heavy cream
- 2 leeks

DIRECTIONS

1. In a saucepan heat olive oil and sauté leek until tender
2. Add remaining ingredients to the saucepan and bring to a boil
3. When all the vegetables are tender transfer to a blender and blend until smooth
4. Pour soup into bowls, garnish with parsley and serve

CARROT SOUP

Serves: **4**

Prep Time: **10**   Minutes

Cook Time: **20**   Minutes

Total Time: **30**   Minutes

INGREDIENTS

- 1 tablespoon olive oil
- 1 lb. carrots
- ¼ red onion
- ½ cup all-purpose flour
- ¼ tsp salt
- ¼ tsp pepper
- 1 can vegetable broth
- 1 cup heavy cream

DIRECTIONS

1. In a saucepan heat olive oil and sauté carrots until tender
2. Add remaining ingredients to the saucepan and bring to a boil
3. When all the vegetables are tender transfer to a blender and blend until smooth
4. Pour soup into bowls, garnish with parsley and serve

CELERY SOUP

Serves: **4**

Prep Time: **10**   Minutes

Cook Time: **20**   Minutes

Total Time: **30**   Minutes

INGREDIENTS

- 1 tablespoon olive oil
- ¼ red onion
- ½ cup all-purpose flour
- ¼ tsp salt
- ¼ tsp pepper
- 1 can vegetable broth
- 1 cup heavy cream
- 1 cup celery

DIRECTIONS

1. In a saucepan heat olive oil and sauté onion until tender
2. Add remaining ingredients to the saucepan and bring to a boil
3. When all the vegetables are tender transfer to a blender and blend until smooth
4. Pour soup into bowls, garnish with parsley and serve

GREEN PESTO PASTA

Serves: 2

Prep Time: 5   Minutes

Cook Time: 15   Minutes

Total Time: 20   Minutes

INGREDIENTS

- 4 oz. spaghetti
- 2 cups basil leaves
- 2 garlic cloves
- ¼ cup olive oil
- 2 tablespoons parmesan cheese
- ½ tsp black pepper

DIRECTIONS

1. Bring water to a boil and add pasta
2. In a blend add parmesan cheese, basil leaves, garlic and blend
3. Add olive oil, pepper and blend again
4. Pour pesto onto pasta and serve when ready

Serves: **2**

Prep Time: **10**   Minutes

Cook Time: **10**   Minutes

Total Time: **20**   Minutes

INGREDIENTS

- 3 oz. shrimp
- ½ cup zucchini
- ½ cup fiesta garden salsa
- ½ oz. Monterey Jack cheese
- cilantro
- 1 tortilla

DIRECTIONS

1. In a bowl add zucchini, shrimp and salsa
2. Microwave for 4-5 minutes, remove and add grated cheese
3. Sprinkle cilantro and pour mixture over tortilla
4. Serve when ready

DIJON VINAIGRETTE

Serves: 2

Prep Time: 5   Minutes

Cook Time: 5   Minutes

Total Time: 10   Minutes

INGREDIENTS

- 2 tablespoons red wine vinegar
- 1 tablespoon water
- 1 tablespoon olive oil
- 1 tsp Dijon mustard
- ½ tsp garlic powder

DIRECTIONS

1. In a bowl mix all ingredients
2. Chill overnight and serve

COTTAGE CHEESE CASSEROLE

Serves: **3**

Prep Time: **10** Minutes

Cook Time: **50** Minutes

Total Time: **60** Minutes

INGREDIENTS

- 2 eggs
- 2 cups cottage cheese
- 1 red onion
- 1 pinch of pepper

DIRECTIONS

1. In a bowl mix all ingredients and pour into a casserole dish
2. Bake at 325 for 50 minutes
3. Remove and serve

FRENCH DRESSING

Serves: **2**

Prep Time: **5**   Minutes

Cook Time: **5**   Minutes

Total Time: **10** Minutes

INGREDIENTS

- ½ cup ketchup
- ¼ cup oil
- ¼ cup white vinegar
- 1 tsp lemon juice
- dash of pepper

DIRECTIONS

1. In a bowl mix all ingredients
2. Chill overnight and serve

TAPENADE

Serves: **4**
Prep Time: **10**   Minutes

Cook Time: **10**   Minutes

Total Time: **20**   Minutes

INGREDIENTS

- ½ cup Kalamata olives
- 1 tsp capers
- ½ cup olive oil
- 1 tablespoon balsamic vinegar

DIRECTIONS

1. In a bowl chop olive and mix with crushed garlic
2. Add the rest of ingredients and mix well
3. Chill for 1-2 hours serve with asparagus or vegetables

MUSHROOM BACON

Serves: *3*
Prep Time: *10*   Minutes

Cook Time: *10*   Minutes

Total Time: *20*   Minutes

INGREDIENTS

- 1 tablespoon oil
- 1 packet Portobello mushroom
- ½ cup maple syrup
- 1 tablespoon liquid smoke
- pinch of salt
- pinch of pepper

DIRECTIONS

1. In a bowl mix marinate the mushroom slices, mix with liquid smoke, maple syrup salt, and pepper
2. Cut the mushrooms into strips and marinade for 12-15 minutes
3. In a skillet cook mushrooms for 3-5 minutes or until browned
4. Remove, add lettuce, sliced tomato and serve

ZUCCHINI CASSEROLE

Serves: **4**

Prep Time: **10**   Minutes

Cook Time: **1**   Hour 30 Minutes

Total Time: **1**   Hour 30 Minutes

INGREDIENTS

- 2 lb. zucchini
- 1 onion
- ½ cup rice
- 1 can mushroom soup
- 2 beaten eggs
- 2 tablespoons butter
- 1 cup cheddar cheese

DIRECTIONS

1. Preheat the oven 325 F
2. In a bowl mix all ingredients
3. Pour mixture into a casserole dish
4. Top with grated cheese

NOODLES WITH PARMESAN CHEESE

Serves: **4**

Prep Time: **10** Minutes

Cook Time: **30** Minutes

Total Time: **40** Minutes

INGREDIENTS

- 1 lb. noodles
- 1 cup parmesan cheese
- 2 cloves garlic
- 3 tablespoons coriander
- 5 tablespoons olive oil
- ¾ tsp salt
- ¼ tsp pepper

DIRECTIONS

1. Cook noodles according to directions and place in a bowl
2. Chop coriander and place in a bowl with crushed garlic
3. Mix with remaining ingredients, stir into the noodles
4. Serve when ready

BALSAMIC CHICKEN

Serves: **4**

Prep Time: **10**   Minutes

Cook Time: **2**   Hours 30 Minutes

Total Time: **2**   Hours 40 Hours

INGREDIENTS

- 3 chicken breasts
- ¼ cup olive oil
- ¼ cup balsamic vinegar
- 1 clove garlic

DIRECTIONS

1. In a bowl, add all ingredients
2. Add chicken and marinade for 3-4 hours
3. Grill and serve with vegetables

STEAMED SALMON

Serves: **4**

Prep Time: **10** Minutes

Cook Time: **30** Minutes

Total Time: **40** Minutes

INGREDIENTS

- 3 salmon fillets
- ½ tsp dill weed
- ½ tsp parsley
- salt

DIRECTIONS

1. Season the salmon with pepper and parsley
2. Place each fillet on the grill at 325 F for 30 minutes
3. Remove and serve with vegetables

ROASTED POTATOES

Serves: **4**

Prep Time: **10** Minutes

Cook Time: **20** Minutes

Total Time: **30** Minutes

INGREDIENTS

- 1 red potato wedges
- 1 tablespoon rosemary
- 2 garlic cloves
- 1 tablespoon olive oil
- ¼ tsp onion powder
- ½ tsp salt
- ½ tsp pepper

DIRECTIONS

1. In a bowl mix potato wedges and the rest of the ingredients
2. Toss to coat the potato wedges and place on a baking sheet
3. Bake for 20-25 minutes or until tender
4. Remove and serve

FRESH SALAD

Serves: *1*
Prep Time: 5   Minutes

Cook Time: 5   Minutes

Total Time: *10*   Minutes

INGREDIENTS

- 1 lb beef
- 1 package taco seasoning
- 1 iceberg lettuce
- 3 tomatoes
- 1 cup cheese
- 1/3 cup corn
- 1 bunch scallions

DIRECTIONS

1. Brown the beef, then season
2. In a bowl mix all ingredients and mix well
3. Serve with dressing

CHICKEN SALAD

Serves: **6**

Prep Time: **5**   Minutes

Cook Time: **5**   Minutes

Total Time: **10**   Minutes

INGREDIENTS

- 3 cups chicken
- 1 cup pecans
- ½ cup Greek yogurt
- 3 celery stalks
- 1/3 cup mayonnaise
- 3 tsp mustard
- 2 tsp vinegar
- 1 tsp salt
- Black pepper
- 1/3 cup red onion
- ¼ cup parsley

DIRECTIONS

1. Toast the pecans
2. Cook the chicken
3. Allow the pecans to cool, then chop

4. In a bowl mix all ingredients and mix well
5. Serve with dressing

CRANBERRY PECAN SALAD

Serves: 2

Prep Time: 5   Minutes

Cook Time: 5   Minutes

Total Time: 10   Minutes

INGREDIENTS

- 1 cup cooked chicken breast
- 1 tablespoon pecans
- 2 tablespoons cranberries
- ¼ cup red onion
- 2 tablespoons Greek yogurt
- 1 tsp dried thyme
- 1 cup salad dressing

DIRECTIONS

1. In a bowl combine all ingredients together and mix well
2. Serve with dressing

PEAR SALAD

Serves: **2**

Prep Time: **5**   Minutes

Cook Time: **5**   Minutes

Total Time: **10**   Minutes

INGREDIENTS

- 4 cups romaine lettuce
- 2 pears
- ½ cup cranberries
- ¼ cup pecans
- ¼ cup red onion
- 4 slices turkey bacon
- ¼ cup cheese

DIRECTIONS

1. In a bowl combine all ingredients together and mix well
2. Serve with dressing

WATERMELON SALAD

Serves: **2**

Prep Time: **5**   Minutes

Cook Time: **5**   Minutes

Total Time: ***10***   Minutes

INGREDIENTS

- **5 cups watermelon**
- **½ cup feta cheese**
- **¼ red onion**
- **¼ black olives**
- **3 tablespoons rice vinegar**

DIRECTIONS

1. **In a bowl combine all ingredients together and mix well**
2. **Serve with dressing**

Serves: **2**

Prep Time: **5**   Minutes

Cook Time: **5**   Minutes

Total Time: **10**   Minutes

INGREDIENTS

- **4 cups white potato**
- **1 pinch salt**
- **2 tablespoons olive oil**
- **¼ cup corn**
- **½ cup black beans**
- **2 tablespoons lemon juice**

DIRECTIONS

1. **In a bowl combine all ingredients together and mix well**
2. **Serve with dressing**

SOUTHWESTERN SALAD

Serves: 2

Prep Time: 5   Minutes

Cook Time: 5   Minutes

Total Time: 10   Minutes

INGREDIENTS

- 4 cups cooked white potato
- 2 tablespoons olive oil
- ¼ cup red bell pepper
- ¼ cup red onion
- ½ cup corn
- ¼ cup cilantro
- 1 tsp garlic
- 1 cup salad dressing

DIRECTIONS

1. In a bowl combine all ingredients together and mix well
2. Serve with dressing

Serves: **2**

Prep Time: **5**   Minutes

Cook Time: **5**   Minutes

Total Time: **10**   Minutes

INGREDIENTS

- 2 cups watermelon
- ¼ red onion
- ¼ cup fete cheese
- 2 cups tomatoes
- 1 tablespoon basil
- 1 cup salad dressing

DIRECTIONS

1. **In a bowl combine all ingredients together and mix well**
2. **Serve with dressing**

MELON SALAD

Serves: **2**

Prep Time: **5**   Minutes

Cook Time: **5**   Minutes

Total Time: **10** Minutes

INGREDIENTS

- 1 package baby spinach
- 1 cup cantaloupe
- 1 cucumber
- 1 cup red onion
- 2 tablespoons honey

DIRECTIONS

1. In a bowl combine all ingredients together and mix well
2. Serve with dressing

RED CABBAGE FRITATTA

Serves: **2**

Prep Time: **10** Minutes

Cook Time: **20** Minutes

Total Time: **30** Minutes

INGREDIENTS

- ½ lb. red cabbage
- 1 tablespoon olive oil
- ½ red onion
- 2 eggs
- ¼ tsp salt
- 2 oz. cheddar cheese
- 1 garlic clove
- ¼ tsp dill

DIRECTIONS

1. In a bowl whisk eggs with salt and cheese
2. In a frying pan heat olive oil and pour egg mixture
3. Add remaining ingredients and mix well
4. Serve when ready

KALE FRITATTA

Serves: **2**

Prep Time: **10** Minutes

Cook Time: **20** Minutes

Total Time: **30** Minutes

INGREDIENTS

- 1 cup kale
- 1 tablespoon olive oil
- ½ red onion
- ¼ tsp salt
- 2 eggs
- 2 oz. cheddar cheese
- 1 garlic clove
- ¼ tsp dill

DIRECTIONS

1. In a skillet sauté kale until tender
2. In a bowl whisk eggs with salt and cheese
3. In a frying pan heat olive oil and pour egg mixture
4. Add remaining ingredients and mix well
5. When ready serve with sautéed kale

BRUSSEL SPROUTS FRITATTA

Serves: **2**

Prep Time: **10**   Minutes

Cook Time: **20**   Minutes

Total Time: **30**   Minutes

INGREDIENTS

- 1 cup brussel sprouts
- 1 tablespoon olive oil
- ½ red onion
- ¼ tsp salt
- 2 eggs
- 2 oz. parmesan cheese
- 1 garlic clove
- ¼ tsp dill

DIRECTIONS

1. In a bowl whisk eggs with salt and cheese
2. In a frying pan heat olive oil and pour egg mixture
3. Add remaining ingredients and mix well
4. Serve when ready

BROCCOLI FRITATTA

Serves: **2**

Prep Time: **10** Minutes

Cook Time: **20** Minutes

Total Time: **30** Minutes

INGREDIENTS

- 1 cup broccoli
- 1 tablespoon olive oil
- ½ red onion
- ¼ tsp salt
- 2 eggs
- 2 oz. cheddar cheese
- 1 garlic clove
- ¼ tsp dill

DIRECTIONS

1. In a skillet sauté broccoli until tender
2. In a bowl whisk eggs with salt and cheese
3. In a frying pan heat olive oil and pour egg mixture
4. Add remaining ingredients and mix well
5. When ready serve with sautéed broccoli

SPAGHETI SQUASH

Serves: 2

Prep Time: 5   Minutes

Cook Time: 15   Minutes

Total Time: 20   Minutes

INGREDIENTS

- 1 spaghetti squash

DIRECTIONS

1. Cut the spaghetti squash in half and remove seeds
2. Spiralize the squash and set aside
3. Fill a container with water and place the squash side down in a container
4. Microwave for 5-6 minutes
5. Serve when ready

SPICY MUSSELS

Serves: **4**

Prep Time: **10** Minutes

Cook Time: **20** Minutes

Total Time: **30** Minutes

INGREDIENTS

- 2 shallots
- 2 garlic cloves
- 2 tablespoons chilies
- 1 cup water
- 2 tablespoon soy sauce
- 2 lb. mussels

DIRECTIONS

1. Place all ingredients in a pot and bring to a boil
2. Simmer on medium heat for 12-15 minutes
3. Cover with a lid and cook until mussels cover up
4. Serve when ready

SHRIMP FAJITAS

Serves:	**4**
Prep Time:	**10** Minutes
Cook Time:	**20** Minutes
Total Time:	**30** Minutes

INGREDIENTS

- 2 tsp Chile powder
- 2 tsp salt
- 1 tsp cumin
- 1 tsp onion powder
- 2 tablespoons lime juice
- 2 lb. shrimp
- 1 green pepper
- 1 red onion

DIRECTIONS

1. Mix all spices together and place fajita aside
2. Toss the shrimp with fajita seasoning and let marinate for a couple of minutes
3. In a skillet heat oil and cook shrimp until soft
4. When ready remove from the skillet and serve

GARLIC CLAMS

Serves: **2**

Prep Time: **10** Minutes

Cook Time: **20** Minutes

Total Time: **30** Minutes

INGREDIENTS

- 1 cup water
- 2 tablespoons lemon juice
- 2 garlic cloves
- 1 tsp thyme
- 1 lb. clams
- ¼ tsp salt

DIRECTIONS

1. In a skillet heat olive oil and sauté garlic, onion and thyme for 4-5 minutes
2. Add water, salt, lemon juice and clams
3. Cover with a lid and cook until shells open up
4. Serve when ready

CROCKPOT CHICKEN

Serves: **6-8**

Prep Time: **10**   Minutes

Cook Time: 5   Hours

Total Time: 5   Hours 10 Minutes

INGREDIENTS

- 1 chicken
- 1 tsp paprika
- 1 tsp salt
- 1 tsp pepper
- 1 tsp garlic powder
- 1 tsp basil
- 1 tsp oregano
- 4-5 lemon slices
- 4-5 potato slices

DIRECTIONS

1. Mix all spices together and rub the chicken with the mixture
2. Stuff the chicken with lemon and potato slices
3. Place the chicken into the slow cooker and cook on medium for 4-5 hours
4. When ready remove from the slow cooker and serve

ROASTED SQUASH

Serves: **3-4**

Prep Time: **10** Minutes

Cook Time: **20** Minutes

Total Time: **30** Minutes

INGREDIENTS

- 2 delicata squashes
- 2 tablespoons olive oil
- 1 tsp curry powder
- 1 tsp salt

DIRECTIONS

1. Preheat the oven to 400 F
2. Cut everything in half lengthwise
3. Toss everything with olive oil and place onto a prepared baking sheet
4. Roast for 18-20 minutes at 400 F or until golden brown
5. When ready remove from the oven and serve

CUCUMBER CHIPS

Serves: **2**

Prep Time: **10**   Minutes

Cook Time: **20**   Minutes

Total Time: **30**   Minutes

INGREDIENTS

- 1 lb. cucumber
- 1 tsp salt
- 1 tsp smoked paprika
- 1 tablespoon olive oil

DIRECTIONS

1. Preheat the oven to 425 F
2. In a bowl toss everything with olive oil and seasoning
3. Spread everything onto a prepared baking sheet
4. Bake for 8-10 minutes or until crisp
5. When ready remove from the oven and serve

Serves: **2**
Prep Time: **10**   Minutes

Cook Time: **20**   Minutes

Total Time: **30**   Minutes

INGREDIENTS

- 1 lb. squash
- 1 tsp salt
- 1 tsp smoked paprika
- 1 tablespoon olive oil

DIRECTIONS

1. Preheat the oven to 425 F
2. In a bowl toss everything with olive oil and seasoning
3. Spread everything onto a prepared baking sheet
4. Bake for 8-10 minutes or until crisp
5. When ready remove from the oven and serve

PIZZA

ZUCCHINI PIZZA

Serves: *6-8*

Prep Time: *10*   Minutes

Cook Time: *15*   Minutes

Total Time: *25*   Minutes

INGREDIENTS

- 1 pizza crust
- ½ cup tomato sauce
- ¼ black pepper
- 1 cup zucchini slices
- 1 cup mozzarella cheese
- 1 cup olives

DIRECTIONS

1. Spread tomato sauce on the pizza crust
2. Place all the toppings on the pizza crust
3. Bake the pizza at 425 F for 12-15 minutes
4. When ready remove pizza from the oven and serve

CHICKEN PIZZA

Serves: **2**

Prep Time: **10**   Minutes

Cook Time: **20**   Minutes

Total Time: **30**   Minutes

INGREDIENTS

- 1 ready-made pizza crust
- 1 tsp olive oil
- 1 cup onion
- 14 cup red pepper strips
- 1 cup chicken
- ¼ cup barbecue sauce
- 1 cup mozzarella cheese
- topping of any choice

DIRECTIONS

1. Preheat the oven to 425 F
2. In a frying pan add pepper strips, onion, chicken and cook on low heat
3. Cook until ready and remove from heat
4. Place crust on a cookie sheet and spread barbecue sauce, and the rest of ingredients on the crust
5. Top with mozzarella and bake for 12-15 minutes

Serves: 2

Prep Time: *10*   Minutes

Cook Time: *20*   Minutes

Total Time: *30*   Minutes

INGREDIENTS

- 1 loaf ciabatta
- 1 cup tomato sauce
- 1 zucchini
- ½ cup mushrooms
- 1 cup mozzarella cheese
- 1 tablespoon basil

DIRECTIONS

1. Preheat the oven to 375 F
2. Cum ciabatta lengthwise and place on a cookie sheet
3. Spread sauce, zucchini, mushrooms on each one and top with mozzarella
4. Sprinkle basil, bake for 12-15 minutes, remove and serve

SHRIMP PIZZA

Serves: **2**

Prep Time: **10** Minutes

Cook Time: **20** Minutes

Total Time: **30** Minutes

INGREDIENTS

- 13 oz. pizza dough
- 1 tablespoon cornmeal
- ¼ cup ricotta cheese
- 1 lb. shrimp
- 5 cloves garlic
- 1 cup mozzarella cheese
- 1 tablespoon dried basil

DIRECTIONS

1. Preheat the oven to 375 F
2. In a baking pan sprinkle cornmeal and add the pizza dough, bake for 6-8 minutes
3. Remove and cover pizza with mozzarella, ricotta, garlic and sprinkle with basil
4. Bake for 12-15 minutes, remove and serve

THIRD COOKBOOK

APPLES PANCAKES

Serves: **4**

Prep Time: **10** Minutes

Cook Time: **20** Minutes

Total Time: **30** Minutes

INGREDIENTS

- 1 cup whole wheat flour
- ¼ tsp baking soda
- ¼ tsp baking powder
- 1 cup apples
- 2 eggs
- 1 cup milk

DIRECTIONS

1. In a bowl combine all ingredients together and mix well
2. In a skillet heat olive oil
3. Pour ¼ of the batter and cook each pancake for 1-2 minutes per side
4. When ready remove from heat and serve

BREADFRUIT PANCAKES

Serves: **4**

Prep Time: **10**   Minutes

Cook Time: **30**   Minutes

Total Time: **40**   Minutes

INGREDIENTS

- 1 cup whole wheat flour
- ¼ tsp baking soda
- ¼ tsp baking powder
- 1 cup breadfruit
- 2 eggs
- 1 cup milk

DIRECTIONS

1. In a bowl combine all ingredients together and mix well
2. In a skillet heat olive oil
3. Pour ¼ of the batter and cook each pancake for 1-2 minutes per side
4. When ready remove from heat and serve

COCONUT PANCAKES

Serves: **4**

Prep Time: **10**   Minutes

Cook Time: **20**   Minutes

Total Time: **30**   Minutes

INGREDIENTS

- 1 cup whole wheat flour
- ¼ tsp baking soda
- ¼ tsp baking powder
- 1 cup coconut flakes
- 2 eggs
- 1 cup milk

DIRECTIONS

1. In a bowl combine all ingredients together and mix well
2. In a skillet heat olive oil
3. Pour ¼ of the batter and cook each pancake for 1-2 minutes per side
4. When ready remove from heat and serve

STRAWBERRY PANCAKES

Serves: *4*
Prep Time: *10*   Minutes

Cook Time: *20*   Minutes

Total Time: *30*   Minutes

INGREDIENTS

- 1 cup whole wheat flour
- ¼ tsp baking soda
- ¼ tsp baking powder
- 1 cup strawberries
- 2 eggs
- 1 cup milk

DIRECTIONS

1. In a bowl combine all ingredients together and mix well
2. In a skillet heat olive oil
3. Pour ¼ of the batter and cook each pancake for 1-2 minutes per side
4. When ready remove from heat and serve

Serves: **4**

Prep Time: **10** Minutes

Cook Time: **30** Minutes

Total Time: **40** Minutes

INGREDIENTS

- 1 cup whole wheat flour
- ¼ tsp baking soda
- ¼ tsp baking powder
- 2 eggs
- 1 cup milk

DIRECTIONS

1. In a bowl combine all ingredients together and mix well
2. In a skillet heat olive oil
3. Pour ¼ of the batter and cook each pancake for 1-2 minutes per side
4. When ready remove from heat and serve

SPINACH OMELETTE

Serves: **1**

Prep Time: **5** Minutes

Cook Time: **10** Minutes

Total Time: **15** Minutes

INGREDIENTS

- 2 eggs
- ¼ tsp salt
- ¼ tsp black pepper
- 1 tablespoon olive oil
- ¼ cup cheese
- ¼ tsp basil
- 1 cup spinach

DIRECTIONS

1. In a bowl combine all ingredients together and mix well
2. In a skillet heat olive oil and pour the egg mixture
3. Cook for 1-2 minutes per side
4. When ready remove omelette from the skillet and serve

ZUCCHINI OMELETTE

Serves: **1**

Prep Time: **5**   Minutes

Cook Time: **10**   Minutes

Total Time: **15**   Minutes

INGREDIENTS

- 2 eggs
- ¼ tsp salt
- ¼ tsp black pepper
- 1 tablespoon olive oil
- ¼ cup cheese
- ¼ tsp basil
- 1 cup zucchini

DIRECTIONS

1. In a bowl combine all ingredients together and mix well
2. In a skillet heat olive oil and pour the egg mixture
3. Cook for 1-2 minutes per side
4. When ready remove omelette from the skillet and serve

SHALLOT OMELETTE

Serves: **1**

Prep Time: **5**   Minutes

Cook Time: **10** Minutes

Total Time: **15** Minutes

INGREDIENTS

- 2 eggs
- ¼ tsp salt
- ¼ tsp black pepper
- 1 tablespoon olive oil
- ¼ cup cheese
- ¼ tsp basil
- 1 cup shallot

DIRECTIONS

1. In a bowl combine all ingredients together and mix well
2. In a skillet heat olive oil and pour the egg mixture
3. Cook for 1-2 minutes per side
4. When ready remove omelette from the skillet and serve

MUSHROOM OMELETTE

Serves: **1**
Prep Time: **5**   Minutes

Cook Time: **10**   Minutes

Total Time: **15**   Minutes

INGREDIENTS

- 2 eggs
- ¼ tsp salt
- ¼ tsp black pepper
- 1 tablespoon olive oil
- ¼ cup cheese
- ¼ tsp basil
- 1 cup mushrooms

DIRECTIONS

1. In a bowl combine all ingredients together and mix well
2. In a skillet heat olive oil and pour the egg mixture
3. Cook for 1-2 minutes per side
4. When ready remove omelette from the skillet and serve

PARMESAN OMELETTE

Serves: *1*

Prep Time: *5*   Minutes

Cook Time: *10*   Minutes

Total Time: *15*   Minutes

INGREDIENTS

- 2 eggs
- ¼ tsp salt
- ¼ tsp black pepper
- 1 tablespoon olive oil
- ¼ cup cheese
- ¼ tsp basil
- 1 cup parmesan cheese

DIRECTIONS

1. In a bowl combine all ingredients together and mix well
2. In a skillet heat olive oil and pour the egg mixture
3. Cook for 1-2 minutes per side
4. When ready remove omelette from the skillet and serve

BANANA PANCAKES

Serves: *4*

Prep Time: *10* Minutes

Cook Time: *20* Minutes

Total Time: *30* Minutes

INGREDIENTS

- 1 cup whole wheat flour
- ¼ tsp baking soda
- ¼ tsp baking powder
- 1 cup mashed banana
- 2 eggs
- 1 cup milk

DIRECTIONS

1. In a bowl combine all ingredients together and mix well
2. In a skillet heat olive oil
3. Pour ¼ of the batter and cook each pancake for 1-2 minutes per side
4. When ready remove from heat and serve

Serves: **4**

Prep Time: **10** Minutes

Cook Time: **30** Minutes

Total Time: **40** Minutes

INGREDIENTS

- 1 cup whole wheat flour
- ¼ tsp baking soda
- ¼ tsp baking powder
- 1 cup pear
- 2 eggs
- 1 cup milk

DIRECTIONS

1. In a bowl combine all ingredients together and mix well
2. In a skillet heat olive oil
3. Pour ¼ of the batter and cook each pancake for 1-2 minutes per side
4. When ready remove from heat and serve

CHERRIES PANCAKES

Serves: **4**

Prep Time: **10** Minutes

Cook Time: **20** Minutes

Total Time: **30** Minutes

INGREDIENTS

- 1 cup whole wheat flour
- ¼ tsp baking soda
- ¼ tsp baking powder
- 1 cup cherries
- 2 eggs
- 1 cup milk

DIRECTIONS

1. In a bowl combine all ingredients together and mix well
2. In a skillet heat olive oil
3. Pour ¼ of the batter and cook each pancake for 1-2 minutes per side
4. When ready remove from heat and serve

RAISIN PANCAKES

Serves: **4**

Prep Time: **10**   Minutes

Cook Time: **20**   Minutes

Total Time: **30**   Minutes

INGREDIENTS

- 1 cup whole wheat flour
- ¼ tsp baking soda
- ¼ tsp baking powder
- ½ cup raisins
- 2 eggs
- 1 cup milk

DIRECTIONS

1. In a bowl combine all ingredients together and mix well
2. In a skillet heat olive oil
3. Pour ¼ of the batter and cook each pancake for 1-2 minutes per side
4. When ready remove from heat and serve

NUTS PANCAKES

Serves: **4**
Prep Time: **10**   Minutes

Cook Time: **30**   Minutes

Total Time: **40**   Minutes

INGREDIENTS

- 1 cup whole wheat flour
- ¼ tsp baking soda
- ¼ tsp baking powder
- 2 eggs
- 1 cup milk
- ½ cup nuts

DIRECTIONS

1. In a bowl combine all ingredients together and mix well
2. In a skillet heat olive oil
3. Pour ¼ of the batter and cook each pancake for 1-2 minutes per side
4. When ready remove from heat and serve

GUAVA MUFFINS

Serves:	**8-12**	
Prep Time:	**10**	Minutes
Cook Time:	**20**	Minutes
Total Time:	**30**	Minutes

INGREDIENTS

- 2 eggs
- 1 tablespoon olive oil
- 1 cup milk
- 2 cups whole wheat flour
- 1 tsp baking soda
- ¼ tsp baking soda
- 1 cup guava
- 1 tsp cinnamon
- ¼ cup molasses

DIRECTIONS

1. In a bowl combine all wet ingredients
2. In another bowl combine all dry ingredients
1. Combine wet and dry ingredients together
2. Pour mixture into 8-12 prepared muffin cups, fill 2/3 of the cups
3. Bake for 18-20 minutes at 375 F

POMEGRANATE MUFFINS

Serves: **8-12**

Prep Time: **10** Minutes

Cook Time: **20** Minutes

Total Time: **30** Minutes

INGREDIENTS

- 2 eggs
- 1 tablespoon olive oil
- 1 cup milk
- 2 cups whole wheat flour
- 1 tsp baking soda
- ¼ tsp baking soda
- 1 tsp cinnamon
- 1 cup mashed pomegranate

DIRECTIONS

1. In a bowl combine all wet ingredients
2. In another bowl combine all dry ingredients
3. Combine wet and dry ingredients together
4. Pour mixture into 8-12 prepared muffin cups, fill 2/3 of the cups
5. Bake for 18-20 minutes at 375 F
6. When ready remove from the oven and serve

PAPAYA MUFFINS

Serves: *8-12*
Prep Time: *10*   Minutes
Cook Time: *20*   Minutes
Total Time: *30*   Minutes

INGREDIENTS

- 2 eggs
- 1 tablespoon olive oil
- 1 cup milk
- 2 cups whole wheat flour
- 1 tsp baking soda
- ¼ tsp baking soda
- 1 tsp cinnamon
- 1 cup papaya

DIRECTIONS

1. In a bowl combine all wet ingredients
2. In another bowl combine all dry ingredients
3. Combine wet and dry ingredients together
4. Pour mixture into 8-12 prepared muffin cups, fill 2/3 of the cups
5. Bake for 18-20 minutes at 375 F
6. When ready remove from the oven and serve

PEACH MUFFINS

Serves: **8-12**

Prep Time: **10**   Minutes

Cook Time: **20**   Minutes

Total Time: **30**   Minutes

INGREDIENTS

- 2 eggs
- 1 tablespoon olive oil
- 1 cup milk
- 2 cups whole wheat flour
- 1 tsp baking soda
- ¼ tsp baking soda
- 1 tsp cinnamon
- 1 cup peach

DIRECTIONS

1. In a bowl combine all wet ingredients
2. In another bowl combine all dry ingredients
3. Combine wet and dry ingredients together
4. Pour mixture into 8-12 prepared muffin cups, fill 2/3 of the cups
5. Bake for 18-20 minutes at 375 F
6. When ready remove from the oven and serve

PLUM MUFFINS

Serves: *8-12*
Prep Time: *10*   Minutes

Cook Time: *20*   Minutes

Total Time: *30*   Minutes

INGREDIENTS

- 2 eggs
- 1 tablespoon olive oil
- 1 cup milk
- 2 cups whole wheat flour
- 1 tsp baking soda
- ¼ tsp baking soda
- 1 tsp cinnamon
- 1 cup plums

DIRECTIONS

1. In a bowl combine all wet ingredients
2. In another bowl combine all dry ingredients
3. Combine wet and dry ingredients together
4. Pour mixture into 8-12 prepared muffin cups, fill 2/3 of the cups
5. Bake for 18-20 minutes at 375 F
6. When ready remove from the oven and serve

SIMPLE MUFFINS

Serves: **8-12**

Prep Time: **10**   Minutes

Cook Time: **20**   Minutes

Total Time: **30**   Minutes

INGREDIENTS

- 2 eggs
- 1 tablespoon olive oil
- 1 cup milk
- 2 cups whole wheat flour
- 1 tsp baking soda
- ¼ tsp baking soda
- 1 tsp cinnamon

DIRECTIONS

1. In a bowl combine all wet ingredients
2. In another bowl combine all dry ingredients
3. Combine wet and dry ingredients together
4. Pour mixture into 8-12 prepared muffin cups, fill 2/3 of the cups
5. Bake for 18-20 minutes at 375 F
6. When ready remove from the oven and serve

OMELETTE

Serves: *1*

Prep Time: *5*   Minutes

Cook Time: *10*   Minutes

Total Time: *15*   Minutes

INGREDIENTS

- 2 eggs
- ¼ tsp salt
- ¼ tsp black pepper
- 1 tablespoon olive oil
- ¼ cup cheese
- ¼ tsp basil

DIRECTIONS

1. In a bowl combine all ingredients together and mix well
2. In a skillet heat olive oil and pour the egg mixture
3. Cook for 1-2 minutes per side
4. When ready remove omelette from the skillet and serve

Serves: *1*

Prep Time: 5   Minutes

Cook Time: *10*   Minutes

Total Time: *15*   Minutes

INGREDIENTS

- 2 eggs
- ¼ tsp salt
- ¼ tsp black pepper
- 1 tablespoon olive oil
- ¼ cup cheese
- ¼ tsp basil
- 1 cup zucchini

DIRECTIONS

1. In a bowl combine all ingredients together and mix well
2. In a skillet heat olive oil and pour the egg mixture
3. Cook for 1-2 minutes per side
4. When ready remove omelette from the skillet and serve

TOMATO OMELETTE

Serves: **1**

Prep Time: **5**   Minutes

Cook Time: **10** Minutes

Total Time: **15** Minutes

INGREDIENTS

- 2 eggs
- ¼ tsp salt
- ¼ tsp black pepper
- 1 tablespoon olive oil
- ¼ cup cheese
- ¼ tsp basil
- 1 cup red onion
- 1 tomato

DIRECTIONS

1. In a bowl combine all ingredients together and mix well
2. In a skillet heat olive oil and pour the egg mixture
3. Cook for 1-2 minutes per side
4. When ready remove omelette from the skillet and serve

RED BELL PEPPER OMELETTE

Serves: *1*
Prep Time: *5*   Minutes

Cook Time: *10*   Minutes

Total Time: *15*   Minutes

INGREDIENTS

- 2 eggs
- ¼ tsp salt
- ¼ tsp black pepper
- 1 tablespoon olive oil
- ¼ cup cheese
- ¼ tsp basil
- 1 cup red bell pepper

DIRECTIONS

1. In a bowl combine all ingredients together and mix well
2. In a skillet heat olive oil and pour the egg mixture
3. Cook for 1-2 minutes per side
4. When ready remove omelette from the skillet and serve

BROCCOLI OMELETTE

Serves: **1**

Prep Time: **5**   Minutes

Cook Time: **10**   Minutes

Total Time: **15**   Minutes

INGREDIENTS

- 2 eggs
- ¼ tsp salt
- ¼ tsp black pepper
- 1 tablespoon olive oil
- ¼ cup cheese
- ¼ tsp basil
- 1 cup braccoli

DIRECTIONS

1. In a bowl combine all ingredients together and mix well
2. In a skillet heat olive oil and pour the egg mixture
3. Cook for 1-2 minutes per side
4. When ready remove omelette from the skillet and serve

Serves:	**2**	
Prep Time:	**5**	Minutes
Cook Time:	**30**	Minutes
Total Time:	**35**	Minutes

INGREDIENTS

- 1 tsp vanilla extract
- 1 tablespoon honey
- 1 lb. rolled oats
- 2 tablespoons sesame seeds
- ¼ lb. almonds
- ¼ lb. berries

DIRECTIONS

1. Preheat the oven to 325 F
2. Spread the granola onto a baking sheet
3. Bake for 12-15 minutes, remove and mix everything
4. Bake for another 12-15 minutes or until slightly brown
5. When ready remove from the oven and serve

Serves: **1**

Prep Time: **5** Minutes

Cook Time: **5** Minutes

Total Time: **10** Minutes

INGREDIENTS

- ½ cup dried raisins
- ½ cup dried pecans
- ¼ cup almonds
- 1 cup coconut milk
- 1 tsp cinnamon

DIRECTIONS

1. In a bowl combine all ingredients together
2. Serve with milk

SAUSAGE BREAKFAST SANDWICH

Serves: 2

Prep Time: 5   Minutes

Cook Time: 15   Minutes

Total Time: 20   Minutes

INGREDIENTS

- ¼ cup egg substitute
- 1 muffin
- 1 turkey sausage patty
- 1 tablespoon cheddar cheese

DIRECTIONS

1. In a skillet pour egg and cook on low heat
2. Place turkey sausage patty in a pan and cook for 4-5 minutes per side
3. On a toasted muffin place the cooked egg, top with a sausage patty and cheddar cheese
4. Serve when ready

Serves:	*8-12*
Prep Time:	*10* Minutes
Cook Time:	*20* Minutes
Total Time:	*30* Minutes

INGREDIENTS

- 2 eggs
- 1 tablespoon olive oil
- 1 cup milk
- 2 cups whole wheat flour
- 1 tsp baking soda
- ¼ tsp baking soda
- 1 tsp cinnamon
- 1 cup strawberries

DIRECTIONS

1. In a bowl combine all wet ingredients
2. In another bowl combine all dry ingredients
3. Combine wet and dry ingredients together
4. Pour mixture into 8-12 prepared muffin cups, fill 2/3 of the cups
5. Bake for 18-20 minutes at 375 F
6. When ready remove from the oven and serve

DESSERTS

BREAKFAST COOKIES

Serves: **8-12**

Prep Time: **5** Minutes

Cook Time: **15** Minutes

Total Time: **20** Minutes

INGREDIENTS

- 1 cup rolled oats
- ¼ cup applesauce
- ½ tsp vanilla extract
- 3 tablespoons chocolate chips
- 2 tablespoons dried fruits
- 1 tsp cinnamon

DIRECTIONS

1. Preheat the oven to 325 F
2. In a bowl combine all ingredients together and mix well
3. Scoop cookies using an ice cream scoop
4. Place cookies onto a prepared baking sheet
5. Place in the oven for 12-15 minutes or until the cookies are done
6. When ready remove from the oven and serve

GINGER COLADA SMOOTHIE

Serves: *1*

Prep Time: *5*   Minutes

Cook Time: *5*   Minutes

Total Time: *10* Minutes

INGREDIENTS

- 1 tablespoon ginger
- ½ cup lemon juice
- 1 cup pineapple
- 1 banana
- 1 handful spinach
- 1 handful kale
- 1 cup ice

DIRECTIONS

1. In a blender place all ingredients and blend until smooth
2. Pour smoothie in a glass and serve

RAINBOW SMOOTHIE

Serves: *1*

Prep Time: *5*   Minutes

Cook Time: *5*   Minutes

Total Time: *10*   Minutes

INGREDIENTS

- ¼ cup grapefruit
- ¼ cup watermelon
- 1 cup raspberries
- 1 cup pomegranate
- 1 cup ice

DIRECTIONS

1. In a blender place all ingredients and blend until smooth
2. Pour smoothie in a glass and serve

ACAI SMOOTHIE

Serves: *1*

Prep Time: *5*   Minutes

Cook Time: *5*   Minutes

Total Time: *10*   Minutes

INGREDIENTS

- 1 cup acai puree
- 1 banana
- 1 cup pomegranate juice
- 1 kiwi
- ½ lemon

DIRECTIONS

1. In a blender place all ingredients and blend until smooth
2. Pour smoothie in a glass and serve

BERRY SMOOTHIE

Serves: *1*

Prep Time: *5*   Minutes

Cook Time: *5*   Minutes

Total Time: *10*   Minutes

INGREDIENTS

- 1 cup strawberries
- 1 cup blueberries
- ½ cup orange juice
- ½ cup coconut water
- 1 cup ice

DIRECTIONS

1. In a blender place all ingredients and blend until smooth
2. Pour smoothie in a glass and serve

Serves: *1*

Prep Time: *5*   Minutes

Cook Time: *5*   Minutes

Total Time: *10* Minutes

INGREDIENTS

- 2 stalks celery
- 4 cups spinach
- 1 pear
- 1 banana
- 1 tablespoon lime juice
- 1 cup coconut water
- 1 cup ice

DIRECTIONS

1. In a blender place all ingredients and blend until smooth
2. Pour smoothie in a glass and serve

SUNRISE SMOOTHIE

Serves: *1*

Prep Time: *5*   Minutes

Cook Time: *5*   Minutes

Total Time: *10*   Minutes

INGREDIENTS

- 2 cups kiwi
- 2 bananas
- 2 mangoes
- ½ cup pineapple
- 1 cup ice
- 1 cup coconut water
- 1 tablespoon honey

DIRECTIONS

1. In a blender place all ingredients and blend until smooth
2. Pour smoothie in a glass and serve

SOY SMOOTHIE

Serves: **1**

Prep Time: **5**   Minutes

Cook Time: **5**   Minutes

Total Time: **10**   Minutes

INGREDIENTS

- 2 cups blueberries
- 1 cup soy vanilla yogurt
- 1 cup soy milk
- 1 tsp vanilla essence

DIRECTIONS

1. In a blender place all ingredients and blend until smooth
2. Pour smoothie in a glass and serve

POWER SMOOTHIE

Serves: **1**

Prep Time: **5**   Minutes

Cook Time: **5**   Minutes

Total Time: **10**   Minutes

INGREDIENTS

- 1 cup kale
- ¼ cup greens
- ¼ cup baby spinach
- ¼ cup greens
- ½ cup pineapple
- ½ cup blueberries
- 1 cup almon milk

DIRECTIONS

1. In a blender place all ingredients and blend until smooth
2. Pour smoothie in a glass and serve

OAT SMOOTHIE

Serves: *1*

Prep Time: *5*   Minutes

Cook Time: *5*   Minutes

Total Time: *10*   Minutes

INGREDIENTS

- 1 cup orange juice
- ¼ cup oats
- 1 tablespoon flaxseed meal
- 1 tablespoon honey
- 1 banana
- 1 cup ice

DIRECTIONS

1. In a blender place all ingredients and blend until smooth
2. Pour smoothie in a glass and serve

APPLE SMOOTHIE

Serves: **1**

Prep Time: **5**   Minutes

Cook Time: **5**   Minutes

Total Time: **10**   Minutes

INGREDIENTS

- 2 green apples
- 1 banana
- ½ cup almond milk
- 1 cup ice
- ¼ cup vanilla yogurt
- 1 tsp cinnamon
- ¼ tsp nutmeg

DIRECTIONS

1. In a blender place all ingredients and blend until smooth
2. Pour smoothie in a glass and serve

FOURTH COOKBOOK

CAULIFLOWER STEAKS WITH LEMON SAUCE

Serves: **4**

Prep Time: **10**   Minutes

Cook Time: **10**   Minutes

Total Time: **20**   Minutes

INGREDIENTS

- 1 head cauliflower
- 2 tablespoons olive oil
- 2 tsp paprika

LEMON SAUCE

- 1 cup parsley leaves
- ¼ cup mint leaves
- 1 garlic clove
- ¼ cup olive oil
- ¼ cup green onion
- Juice of 1 lemon

DIRECTIONS

1. In a blender add all ingredients for the lemon sauce and blend until smooth

2. For the cauliflower steak, cut cauliflower into thick slices and rub with olive oil

3. Sprinkle with spices and place the cauliflower in a skillet

4. Cook for 4-5 minutes per side

5. When ready remove and serve with lemon sauce

Serves: **4**

Prep Time: **10** Minutes

Cook Time: **30** Minutes

Total Time: **40** Minutes

INGREDIENTS

- 2 tablespoons olive oil
- salt
- 2 scallions
- ¼ cup cilantro
- 1 head cauliflower
- 1 tablespoon sesame seeds

SAUCE

- 1 tablespoon rice wine vinegar
- 1 tablespoon ginger
- 1 tsp olive oil
- 1 tablespoon soy sauce
- 1 tablespoon hoisin sauce

DIRECTIONS

1. **In a bowl combine all sauce ingredients together and mix well**

2. For the cauliflower heat the olive oil in a skillet and add the cauliflower

3. Add salt, sesame seeds and cook for 4-5 minutes

4. When ready remove from heat, add cilantro and stir to combine

5. Serve with sauce

RICE, KALE AND AVOCADO BOWL

Serves: **2**

Prep Time: **10**   Minutes

Cook Time: **20**   Minutes

Total Time: **30**   Minutes

INGREDIENTS

- 1 cup rice
- 1 garlic clove
- 1 tablespoon rice vinegar
- 2 cups vegetable broth
- pinch of salt
- pinch of pepper
- 2 tablespoons
- 1 bunch kale
- 1 bunch kale
- 1 avocado

DIRECTIONS

1. In a pot stir in broth, rice and garlic
2. Bring to a simmer for and cook until liquid is evaporated
3. When ready toss rice with salt, pepper and vinegar
4. In another books toss kale with olive oil

5. Add kale and avocado slices to the rice
6. Serve when ready

Serves: **4**

Prep Time: **10**   Minutes

Cook Time: **30**   Minutes

Total Time: **40**   Minutes

INGREDIENTS

- ¼ cup red onion
- 1 lb. ground chicken
- 1 tablespoon mustard
- ¼ tsp black pepper
- 1 tablespoon olive oil
- 1 garlic clove
- ¼ cup parsley
- pinch of salt

SAUCE

- 1 cup parsley
- 1 can coconut milk
- 2 scallions
- zest of 1 lemon
- 1 cup ready-made cauliflower rice

DIRECTIONS

1. In a skillet heat olive oil and sauté onion and garlic for 3-4 minutes
2. Remove sautéed onion and garlic to a bowl
3. Stir in parsley, mustard, chicken, seasoning and mix well
4. Form balls from the mixture and place on a baking sheet
5. Bake at 400 F for 20 minutes
6. When ready remove from the oven and set aside
7. In a blender add all ingredients for the sauce and blend
8. Top the meatballs with sauce and cauliflower rice and serve

PINEAPPLE CHICKEN AND LETTUCE WRAPS

Serves: **2**

Prep Time: **10**   Minutes

Cook Time: **20**   Minutes

Total Time: **30**   Minutes

INGREDIENTS

- 2 cups cooked chicken
- 1 tablespoon olive oil
- ¼ tsp paprika
- 1 tablespoon lime juice
- ¼ tsp garlic powder
- ¼ tsp salt
- 1 cup pineapple cubes
- 8 lettuce wraps

DIRECTIONS

1. In a bowl combine garlic powder, lime juice, paprika, olive oil and lime juice
2. In your lettuce wraps add pineapple cubes, chicken and top with lime mixture
3. Serve when ready

Serves: **4**

Prep Time: **10** Minutes

Cook Time: **35** Minutes

Total Time: **45** Minutes

INGREDIENTS

- 1 lb. potatoes
- 1 tsp lemon juice
- 4 salmon fillets
- ¼ tsp paprika
- 2 tablespoons olive oil

DIRECTIONS

1. Bake the potatoes at 375 F for 20-25 minutes
2. Rub the salmon fillets with paprika and olive oil
3. Bake the fish until golden brown
4. When ready from the oven and serve with baked potatoes and lemon juice

GUT ENERGY BOOSTING BOWL

Serves: **1**

Prep Time: **5**   Minutes

Cook Time: **5**   Minutes

Total Time: **10**   Minutes

INGREDIENTS

- 2 cups kale
- 1 tablespoon olive oil
- 1 avocado
- ¼ cup carrot
- ½ cup beans
- ¼ cup cabbage
- 1 cup baked potatoes

DIRECTIONS

1. In a bowl add all ingredients together
2. Drizzle olive oil and salt and mix well
3. Serve when ready

Serves: **2**

Prep Time: **5**   Minutes

Cook Time: **10**   Minutes

Total Time: **15**   Minutes

INGREDIENTS

-   2 zucchinis
-   pinch of salt
-   2 avocados
-   2 tablespoons olive oil
-   2 eggs
-   1 tablespoon olive oil

DIRECTIONS

1. In a bowl toss the zucchini noodles with olive oil
2. Season and transfer to a baking sheet
3. Crack an egg over each portion
4. Bake for 8-10 minutes at 375 F
5. When ready remove from the oven and serve with avocado slices

CHICKEN WITH BAKED VEGGIES

Serves: **4**

Prep Time: **10** Minutes

Cook Time: **30** Minutes

Total Time: **40** Minutes

INGREDIENTS

- 1 tablespoon olive oil
- 1 tablespoon honey
- 2 red bell peppers
- 2 carrots
- ¼ cup parsley
- 1 lb. chicken breast
- 2 onions

DIRECTIONS

1. Place the chicken onto a baking sheet
2. Add the rest of the ingredients to the chicken breast
3. Drizzle olive oil over chicken and veggies
4. Bake at 375 F for 25-30 minutes or until the vegetables are tender
5. When ready remove from the oven and serve

VEGGIE STIR-FRY

Serves: 2

Prep Time: **10**   Minutes

Cook Time: **20**   Minutes

Total Time: **30**   Minutes

INGREDIENTS

- 1 tablespoon cornstarch
- 1 garlic clove
- ¼ cup olive oil
- ¼ head broccoli
- ¼ cup show peas
- ½ cup carrots
- ¼ cup green beans
- 1 tablespoon soy sauce
- ½ cup onion

DIRECTIONS

1. In a bowl combine garlic, olive oil, cornstarch and mix well
2. Add the rest of the ingredients and toss to coat
3. In a skillet cook vegetables mixture until tender
4. When ready transfer to a plate garnish with ginger and serve

GREEK PIZZA

Serves: **6-8**

Prep Time: **10** Minutes

Cook Time: **15** Minutes

Total Time: **25** Minutes

INGREDIENTS

- 1 pizza crust
- 1 tablespoon olive oil
- 6 oz. spinach
- ¼ cup basil
- 1 tsp oregano
- 1 cup mozzarella cheese
- 1 tomato
- ½ cup feta cheese

DIRECTIONS

1. Spread tomato sauce on the pizza crust
2. Place all the toppings on the pizza crust
3. Bake the pizza at 425 F for 12-15 minutes
4. When ready remove pizza from the oven and serve

Serves: **6-8**

Prep Time: **10** Minutes

Cook Time: **15** Minutes

Total Time: **25** Minutes

INGREDIENTS

- 1 cup cooked chicken breast
- ½ cup bbq sauce
- 1 pizza crust
- 1 tablespoon olive oil
- 1 cup cheese
- 1 cup tomatoes

DIRECTIONS

1. Spread tomato sauce on the pizza crust
2. Place all the toppings on the pizza crust
3. Bake the pizza at 425 F for 12-15 minutes
4. When ready remove pizza from the oven and serve

Serves: **1**
Prep Time: **5**   Minutes

Cook Time: **10** Minutes

Total Time: **15** Minutes

INGREDIENTS

- 3 oz. shrimp
- ¼ cup zucchini
- ½ cup fiesta garden salsa
- ¼ oz. cheese
- cilantro
- 1 tortilla

DIRECTIONS

1. In a bowl add zucchini, shrimp and pour salsa over
2. Microwave for 4-5 minutes and sprinkle with grated cheese and cilantro
3. Microwave tortilla for 10-20 seconds and serve with shrimp

CAULIFLOWER FRITTERS

Serves: **8**

Prep Time: **10**   Minutes

Cook Time: **30**   Minutes

Total Time: **40**   Minutes

INGREDIENTS

- 1 head of cauliflower
- ¼ tsp chili powder
- 2 cloves garlic
- 2 tablespoons cilantro
- 1 tsp salt
- ¼ tsp black pepper
- 2 eggs
- 3 tablespoons cornmeal
- ½ cup flour
- 4 tablespoons nutritional yeast

DIRECTIONS

1. Cook cauliflower florets by steaming for 5-6 minutes
2. Mix the cauliflower with chili powder, cilantro, garlic, pepper and salt
3. In another bowl beat the egg, add cauliflower mixture, flour, cornmeal, and yeast

4. Add ¼ cup of the mixture to the pan and press down the fritter
5. Cook until golden brown for 3-4 minutes per side
6. When ready, remove and serve

FRENCH TOAST SANDWICHES

Serves: 2

Prep Time: 5   Minutes

Cook Time: 10   Minutes

Total Time: 15   Minutes

INGREDIENTS

- 4 thin slices bread
- 2 eggs
- 1/3 cup almond milk
- ¼ tsp vanilla extract
- 1 tablespoon cream cheese
- 1 tablespoon apricot preserves
- ½ cup maple syrup

DIRECTIONS

1. In a bowl combine vanilla extract, eggs, almond milk, and mix well
2. Make 2 sandwiches with cream cheese and preserve
3. Place sandwiches in egg mixture on both sides
4. In a skillet cook sandwiches for 2-3 minutes per side or until golden brown
5. When ready remove and serve

GREEK MIXED VEGETABLES

Serves: **6**

Prep Time: **10**   Minutes

Cook Time: **90**   Minutes

Total Time: **100** Minutes

INGREDIENTS

- ½ cup olive oil
- 1 eggplant
- 1 onion
- 2 garlic cloves
- 1 lb. potatoes
- 5 tomatoes
- 10 cherry tomatoes
- 1 cup tomato passata
- 1 cup water
- 1 tablespoon dried oregano
- 1 tablespoon parsley
- 1 tsp salt

DIRECTIONS

1. Preheat the oven to 400 F
2. In a frying pan add olive oil, eggplant and cook for 6-7 minutes

3. Add garlic, onion and sauté for 5-6 minutes

4. Add potato, zucchini, passata, tomatoes, and water

5. Sprinkle with oregano, parsley, pepper, and salt

6. Mix well and transfer to a baking dish, drizzle with olive oil and bake for 45-55 minutes or until the top has browned

7. When ready remove and serve

GRILLED SALMON STEAKS

Serves: **4**

Prep Time: **5** Minutes

Cook Time: **15** Minutes

Total Time: **20** Minutes

INGREDIENTS

- 2 salmon steaks
- 2 tablespoons dipping sauce
- 1 tsp cooking oil

DIRECTIONS

1. Heat grill and rub with cooking oil
2. Baste steaks with sauce
3. Cook for 4-5 minutes per side
4. Don't overcook
5. When ready remove and serve

Serves: **8**

Prep Time: **10**   Minutes

Cook Time: **90**   Minutes

Total Time: **100**   Minutes

INGREDIENTS

- ¼ cup green beans
- ¼ cup snow peas
- 1 cup cauliflower florets
- 1 cup water chestnuts
- 2 radishes
- 2 scallions
- ½ cup red onion
- 1 tsp powdered ginger
- ½ cup rice wine vinegar

DIRECTIONS

1. In a bowl combine cauliflower floret, radish slices, onions, water chestnuts and mix well
2. In another bowl combine rice wine vinegar, powdered ginger and pour over vegetables
3. Refrigerate for 1-2 hours
4. When ready remove and serve

BROCCOLI CASSEROLE

Serves: **4**

Prep Time: **10**   Minutes

Cook Time: **15**   Minutes

Total Time: **25**   Minutes

INGREDIENTS

- 1 onion
- 2 chicken breasts
- 2 tablespoons unsalted butter
- 2 eggs
- 2 cups cooked rice
- 2 cups cheese
- 1 cup parmesan cheese
- 2 cups cooked broccoli

DIRECTIONS

1. Sauté the veggies and set aside
2. Preheat the oven to 425 F
3. Transfer the sautéed veggies to a baking dish, add remaining ingredients to the baking dish
4. Mix well, add seasoning and place the dish in the oven
5. Bake for 12-15 minutes or until slightly brown
6. When ready remove from the oven and serve

Serves: **2**

Prep Time: **10**   Minutes

Cook Time: **20**   Minutes

Total Time: **30**   Minutes

INGREDIENTS

- ½ lb. asparagus
- 1 tablespoon olive oil
- ½ red onion
- ¼ tsp salt
- 2 eggs
- 2 oz. cheddar cheese
- 1 garlic clove
- ¼ tsp dill

DIRECTIONS

1. In a bowl whisk eggs with salt and cheese
2. In a frying pan heat olive oil and pour egg mixture
3. Add remaining ingredients and mix well
4. Serve when ready

SPINACH FRITATTA

Serves: **2**

Prep Time: **10**   Minutes

Cook Time: **20**   Minutes

Total Time: **30**   Minutes

INGREDIENTS

- ½ lb. spinach
- 1 tablespoon olive oil
- ½ red onion
- ¼ tsp salt
- 2 eggs
- 2 oz. cheddar cheese
- 1 garlic clove
- ¼ tsp dill

DIRECTIONS

1. In a bowl whisk eggs with salt and cheese
2. In a frying pan heat olive oil and pour egg mixture
3. Add remaining ingredients and mix well
4. Serve when ready

CHEESE FRITATTA

Serves: 2

Prep Time: **10**   Minutes

Cook Time: **20**   Minutes

Total Time: **30**   Minutes

INGREDIENTS

- 1 tablespoon olive oil
- ½ red onion
- ¼ tsp salt
- 2 eggs
- 1 cup cheddar cheese
- 1 garlic clove
- ¼ tsp dill

DIRECTIONS

1. In a bowl whisk eggs with salt and cheese
2. In a frying pan heat olive oil and pour egg mixture
3. Add remaining ingredients and mix well
4. Serve when ready

RHUBARB FRITATTA

Serves: *2*

Prep Time: *10* Minutes

Cook Time: *20* Minutes

Total Time: *30* Minutes

INGREDIENTS

- 1 cup rhubarb
- 1 tablespoon olive oil
- ½ red onion
- ¼ tsp salt
- 2 oz. parmesan cheese
- 1 garlic clove
- ¼ tsp dill

DIRECTIONS

1. In a bowl whisk eggs with salt and parmesan cheese
2. In a frying pan heat olive oil and pour egg mixture
3. Add remaining ingredients and mix well
4. Serve when ready

BROCCOLI FRITATTA

Serves: **2**

Prep Time: **10** Minutes

Cook Time: **20** Minutes

Total Time: **30** Minutes

INGREDIENTS

- 1 cup broccoli
- 1 tablespoon olive oil
- ½ red onion
- 2 eggs
- ¼ tsp salt
- 2 oz. cheddar cheese
- 1 garlic clove
- ¼ tsp dill

DIRECTIONS

1. In a bowl whisk eggs with salt and cheese
2. In a frying pan heat olive oil and pour egg mixture
3. Add remaining ingredients and mix well
4. Serve when ready

TOMATO RISOTTO

Serves: **2**

Prep Time: **10**   Minutes

Cook Time: **25**   Minutes

Total Time: **35**   Minutes

INGREDIENTS

- 2-3 tablespoons olive oil
- 1 red onion
- 1 lb. vine-ripened tomatoes
- 1 lb. risotto rice
- 1 cup vegetable stock
- 1 cup cheese
- 2 oz. basil

DIRECTIONS

1. In a pan heat olive oil and sauté onion until soft
2. Place the tomatoes on a baking tray, drizzle olive oil and roast at 350 F for 18-20 minutes
3. Add the rice, stock to the pan and cook until rice is tender
4. Add the cheese, basil, tomatoes and serve when ready

Serves: **2**

Prep Time: **10** Minutes

Cook Time: **50** Minutes

Total Time: **60** Minutes

INGREDIENTS

- 1 lb. butternut squash
- 3 tablespoons olive oil
- ¼ rolled pastry
- 2 eggs
- 200 ml double cream

DIRECTIONS

1. Roast the squash at 400 F for 18-20 minutes
2. Lay a baking paper on the pastry
3. Top with beans and bake for 12-15 minutes
4. Top the pastry with squash
5. Mix eggs, with double cream and pour over
6. Bake for another 20-25 minutes
7. When ready remove from the oven and serve

TOMATO TARTS

Serves: **2**

Prep Time: **10**   Minutes

Cook Time: **35**   Minutes

Total Time: **45**   Minutes

INGREDIENTS

- 1 lb. pastry
- 2-3 tsp tomato paste
- 1 lb. tomatoes
- 1 tablespoons olive oil
- 1 tablespoon capers
- 1 lb. broccoli

DIRECTIONS

1. Unroll the pastry sheet and cut into rectangles
2. Spread tomato paste over each tart and drizzle olive oil
3. Scatter over capers
4. Bake at 400 F for 18-20 minutes
5. Meanwhile boil the broccoli for 12-15 minutes or until tender
6. When ready remove from the oven and serve with cooked broccoli

Serves: 2

Prep Time: *10*   Minutes

Cook Time: *20*   Minutes

Total Time: *30*   Minutes

INGREDIENTS

- 1 tablespoon olive oil
- 1 onion
- ½ lb. penne pasta
- 2-3 garlic cloves
- 1 oz. parsley
- ½ lb. tomatoes
- ¼ lb. low fat sour cream

DIRECTIONS

1. Heat olive oil in a pan and sauté onion until soft
2. Add pasta, garlic, pasta and water to cover
3. Bring to a boil and simmer for 5-6 minutes
4. Add tomatoes and cook for another 4-5 minutes
5. Drain the pasta mixture and return to the pan
6. Stir in soured cream
7. Garnish with parsley and serve

ROASTED SQUASH

Serves: **3-4**

Prep Time: **10**   Minutes

Cook Time: **20**   Minutes

Total Time: **30**   Minutes

INGREDIENTS

- 2 delicata squashes
- 2 tablespoons olive oil
- 1 tsp curry powder
- 1 tsp salt

DIRECTIONS

1. Preheat the oven to 400 F
2. Cut everything in half lengthwise
3. Toss everything with olive oil and place onto a prepared baking sheet
4. Roast for 18-20 minutes at 400 F or until golden brown
5. When ready remove from the oven and serve

Serves: **2**

Prep Time: **10** Minutes

Cook Time: **20** Minutes

Total Time: **30** Minutes

INGREDIENTS

- 1 lb. brussels sprouts
- 1 tablespoon olive oil
- 1 tablespoon parmesan cheese
- 1 tsp garlic powder
- 1 tsp seasoning

DIRECTIONS

1. Preheat the oven to 425 F
2. In a bowl toss everything with olive oil and seasoning
3. Spread everything onto a prepared baking sheet
4. Bake for 8-10 minutes or until crisp
5. When ready remove from the oven and serve

PASTA

SIMPLE SPAGHETTI

Serves: 2

Prep Time: 5   Minutes

Cook Time: 15   Minutes

Total Time: 20   Minutes

INGREDIENTS

- 10 oz. spaghetti
- 2 eggs
- ½ cup parmesan cheese
- 1 tsp black pepper
- Olive oil
- 1 tsp parsley
- 2 cloves garlic

DIRECTIONS

1. In a pot boil spaghetti (or any other type of pasta), drain and set aside
2. In a bowl whish eggs with parmesan cheese
3. In a skillet heat olive oil, add garlic and cook for 1-2 minutes
4. Pour egg mixture and mix well
5. Add pasta and stir well

6. When ready garnish with parsley and serve

Serves: **2**

Prep Time: **5**   Minutes

Cook Time: **15**   Minutes

Total Time: **20**   Minutes

INGREDIENTS

- ¼ cup mayonnaise
- ¼ cup sweet chili sauce
- 1 tablespoon lime juice
- 1 garlic clove
- 8 z. pasta
- 1 lb. shrimp
- ¼ tsp paprika

DIRECTIONS

1. In a pot boil spaghetti (or any other type of pasta), drain and set aside
2. Place all the ingredients for the sauce in a pot and bring to a simmer
3. Add pasta and mix well
4. When ready garnish with parmesan cheese and serve

PASTA WITH OLIVES AND TOMATOES

Serves: 2

Prep Time: 5   Minutes

Cook Time: 15   Minutes

Total Time: 20   Minutes

INGREDIENTS

- 8 oz. pasta
- 3 tablespoons olive oil
- 2 cloves garlic
- 5-6 anchovy fillets
- 2 cups tomatoes
- 1 cup olives
- ½ cup basil leaves

DIRECTIONS

1. In a pot boil spaghetti (or any other type of pasta), drain and set aside
2. Place all the ingredients for the sauce in a pot and bring to a simmer
3. Add pasta and mix well
4. When ready garnish with parmesan cheese and serve

SALAD

TOMATO AND CUCUMBER SALAD

Serves: **1**
Prep Time: **5**   Minutes
Cook Time: **5**   Minutes
Total Time: **10**   Minutes

INGREDIENTS

- 2 cucumbers
- 2 tomatoes
- 2/3 cup red onion
- ½ cup balsamic vinegar
- ¼ tablespoons white vinegar
- 2 tablespoons olive oil
- basil leaves

DIRECTIONS

1. In a bowl combine all ingredients together and mix well
2. Serve with dressing

Serves: **1**

Prep Time: **5**   Minutes

Cook Time: **5**   Minutes

Total Time: **10** Minutes

INGREDIENTS

- 2 oz. radicchio
- 3 cups shredded romaine
- 8 cherry tomatoes
- 2 stalks celery
- 2 oz. cucumber
- 1 oz. garden cress
- 2 tsp olive oil
- 2 tsp vinegar

DIRECTIONS

1. In a bowl combine all ingredients together and mix well
2. Serve with dressing

BROCCOLI SALAD WITH CRANBERRIES

Serves: **1**

Prep Time: **5**   Minutes

Cook Time: **5**   Minutes

Total Time: **10**   Minutes

INGREDIENTS

- 3 cups broccoli florets
- ½ cup cranberries
- ½ cup sunflower seeds
- 2 apples
- ½ cup red onion
- 1 cup low-fat yoghurt
- ½ cup honey

DIRECTIONS

1. In a bowl combine all ingredients together and mix well
2. Serve with dressing

Serves: **1**

Prep Time: **5** Minutes

Cook Time: **5** Minutes

Total Time: **10** Minutes

INGREDIENTS

- 1 head romaine lettuce
- 4 oz. smoked salmon
- 1 tomato
- 3 radishes
- 1 organic carrot
- ¼ cucumber
- 1 tsp ginger root
- 1 tablespoon canola oil

DIRECTIONS

1. In a bowl combine all ingredients together and mix well
2. Serve with dressing

SHRIMP AND EGGS SALAD

Serves: *1*
Prep Time: 5   Minutes

Cook Time: 5   Minutes

Total Time: *10*   Minutes

INGREDIENTS

- 2 cups shrimp
- ¼ cup cherry tomatoes
- ½ cup mayonnaise
- ½ cup chili sauce
- 2 tablespoons lemon juice
- romaine lettuce
- 2 hard-boiled eggs

DIRECTIONS

1. In a bowl combine all ingredients together and mix well
2. Serve with dressing

Serves: *1*

Prep Time: *5*   Minutes

Cook Time: *5*   Minutes

Total Time: *10* Minutes

INGREDIENTS

- 2 cups arugula leaves
- 2 cups cherry tomatoes
- ½ cup sun-dried tomatoes
- 2 tablespoons olive oil
- 1 tablespoon balsamic vinegar
- 1 avocado

DIRECTIONS

1. In a bowl combine all ingredients together and mix well
2. Serve with dressing

CHICKEN SALAD WITH PINE NUTS

Serves: **1**

Prep Time: **5**   Minutes

Cook Time: **5**   Minutes

Total Time: **10**   Minutes

INGREDIENTS

- 1 lb. chicken breast cooked
- ½ cup red onion
- ¼ cup cucumber
- ¼ cup basil
- ¼ cup cranberries
- 10 oz romaine lettuce

  DRESSING
- 2 tablespoons balsamic vinegar
- 1 tablespoon canola oil
- 1 tablespoon honey
- 1 garlic clove
- salt
- black pepper
- ½ cup pine nuts

DIRECTIONS

1. In a bowl mix all ingredients and mix well
2. Serve with dressing

APPLE SALAD

Serves: **1**

Prep Time: **5** Minutes

Cook Time: **5** Minutes

Total Time: **10** Minutes

INGREDIENTS

- 2 cups cooked chicken
- 1 cup grapes
- ¼ cup celery
- 2 tablespoons red onion
- ¼ cup apples
- 5 tablespoons mayonnaise
- 1 tsp lemon juice
- salt
- lettuce leaves

DIRECTIONS

1. In a bowl mix all ingredients and mix well
2. Serve with dressing

Serves: *1*

Prep Time: 5   Minutes

Cook Time: 5   Minutes

Total Time: *10*   Minutes

INGREDIENTS

- ½ cup raw beets
- ¼ cup carrots
- 1 tablespoon apple juice
- 1 tablespoon olive oil
- ½ tsp ginger
- ¼ tsp salt

DIRECTIONS

1. In a bowl combine all ingredients together and mix well
2. Serve with dressing

THANK YOU FOR READING THIS BOOK!

CPSIA information can be obtained
at www.ICGtesting.com
Printed in the USA
BVHW081913220321
603177BV00006B/326